Illustrations and Written
By Ashlie Urquhart

Copyright Of
Bluce Face Cow

For Iris and Pat

Frankie

Charlie

Alfie

Alfie, Frankie and Charlie were out playing in their garden.

It was a hot sunny summers day.
They were chasing butterflies and bees.

Tom the stray cat was feeling left out
as he walked along the top of the garden fence.

"Come and play Tom" said Alfie,

as Frankie hippity hopped to catch a butterfly
and Charlie pushed his nose up against a flower,
as he watched the bumble bee busily humming on it.

"No" said Tom...angrily!!

Tom started to wobble on the garden fence
and fell to the floor.

As Alfie, Frankie and Charlie watched in horror!!!!!

Tom felt so upset
and embarrassed that he jumped on Charlie's back.
Charlie was so scared that he ran around the garden
with Tom the stray cat on his back.

"Get off Tom" said Alfie and Frankie...
but Charlie was running so fast that Tom couldn't get off.

Tom became so dizzy that he flew off Charlie's back.
And landed in a pile of leaves and mud.

"Are you ok" asked Charlie, all shaken up,
as Tom sat covered in leaves and mud,
with a butterfly on his head.

With that human Mummy Peggy came out into the garden.
"Is everything ok pussy cat". She said

Oh, looks like there has been a bit of a mishap.
"You ok Charlie" said Peggy
"Meow" said Charlie ...
"aaaaw there you go Charlie" as she petted him.

"Hello Tom, you look like you are in a pickle" she said
"Let's help Tom up onto his feet Boys"
"Come on Alfie, Frankie and Charlie.
Looks like there's been a bit of a scrap"
"Come on let's make up and all be friends"

"Let's have some lunch and have a little play"

So, all the cats got themselves together
and relaxed and had a little laugh and made friends..

And all enjoyed their lunch..

Now every lunch time Alfie, Frankie, Charlie and Tom
all have lunch together and have a little play in the Garden.

And Tom the stray cat never felt left out again.
And never got into a scrap with Alfie, Frankie or Charlie again.

THE END

Frankie

Alfie

Charlie

Frankie

Alfie

Charlie

Frankie

Alfie

Charlie

11493748R00016

Printed in Germany
by Amazon Distribution
GmbH, Leipzig